LEGENDARY HEROES
OF THE WILD WEST

DANIEL BOONE
Wilderness Pioneer

William R. Sanford &
Carl R. Green

 Enslow Publishers, Inc.
44 Fadem Road   PO Box 38
Box 699   Aldershot
Springfield, NJ 07081   Hants GU12 6BP
USA   UK

Library of Congress Cataloging-in-Publication Data

Sanford, William R. (William Reynolds), 1927–
    Daniel Boone: wilderness pioneer / William R. Sanford and Carl R. Green.
        p. cm. —(Legendary heroes of the Wild West)
    Includes bibliographical references (p.) and index.
    Summary: Profiles the life and struggles of the renowned wilderness pioneer
Daniel Boone.
    ISBN 0-89490-674-7
    1. Boone, Daniel, 1734–1820—Juvenile literature. 2. Pioneers—Kentucky—
Biography—Juvenile literature. 3. Kentucky—Biography—Juvenile literature.
4. Frontier and pioneer life—Kentucky—Juvenile literature. [1. Boone, Daniel,
1734–1820. 2. Pioneers.] I. Green, Carl R. II. Title. III. Series: Sanford, William R.
(William Reynolds), 1927– Legendary heroes of the Wild West.
    F454.B66S26 1997
    976.9'02'092—dc20

    [B]   96-1991
                                                            CIP
                                                            AC

Printed in the United States of America

10 9 8 7 6 5 4 3 2 1

Photo Credits: Filson Club Historical Society, pp. 8, 12, 15, 16, 19, 25, 36, 40; Kentucky Historical Society, p. 14; William R. Sanford and Carl R. Green, pp. 6, 10, 17, 23, 29, 31, 33; State Historical Society of Wisconsin, p. 37; Washington University Gallery of Art, St. Louis, gift of Nathaniel Phillips, 1890, p. 28.

Cover Illustration: Paul Daly

CONTENTS

AUTHORS' NOTE

For well over a hundred years, the lands west of the Appalachians lay beyond the reach of America's early colonists. The original thirteen colonies held fast to the Atlantic coast. Strict laws, rugged mountains, and fierce Native American tribes blocked movement beyond the Appalachians. Only trappers and traders ventured into what was then the Wild West. Daniel Boone helped break the barriers by opening Kentucky to settlement. This is the true story of how one strong-willed woodsman helped tame a new frontier.

1
DANIEL BOONE
TO THE RESCUE

In July 1776 the American colonies were fighting for their freedom. Patriots clashed with British redcoats in battles up and down the eastern seaboard. In the forests of Kentucky, pioneers faced a different battle. The Cherokee and Shawnee were fighting to evict the white man from their hunting grounds.

Daniel Boone's settlement at Boonesborough was a prime target. A string of peaceful summer days, however, gave a false sense of peace. On Sunday, July 7, three teenage girls slipped away to go canoeing. Daniel's thirteen-year-old daughter, Jemima, took charge of steering. Betsey and Fanny Callaway did the paddling. Back at the settlement, Daniel was taking a nap.

On the far side of the river, a Cherokee chief named Hanging Maw kept watch. Little by little, the current swept the girls' canoe closer to the shore. A Shawnee warrior jumped in and held it fast.

The girls screamed. Fanny, a tiny thirteen-year-old, hit out with her paddle. Betsey, the oldest of the trio at sixteen, joined in. More warriors jumped into the fray. They yanked the paddles away and dragged the girls into the woods. The screaming stopped when a Shawnee threatened to take Betsey's scalp.

Like her father, Jemima was a quick thinker. Pointing to a cut on one bare foot, she told Hanging Maw she could not walk another step. Fanny, too, was barefoot. Hanging Maw told his men to give the two some moccasins. Next, the braves cut off the girls' long dresses at the knees. They did not want their escape to be slowed by skirts catching in the brambles.[1]

Back at Boonesborough, the screams had aroused the settlement. Daniel ran barefoot to the riverbank. For

Out on the Kentucky frontier, a quiet canoe ride could quickly turn tragic. Daniel Boone's daughter Jemima and two friends learned this fact one Sunday afternoon in 1776. A party of Shawnee warriors dragged the canoe to shore and marched the girls into the woods. The Shawnee did not know that Daniel Boone was already organizing a rescue party.

the moment, pursuit was delayed. The only canoe lay on the far side of the river. Twelve-year-old John Gass swam across to retrieve it.

Once they had crossed the river, the trail was easy to find. The girls had dropped bits of cloth and broken twigs as they trudged along. While Daniel studied the signs, Richard Callaway and a party of horsemen joined him. The riders were eager to chase the kidnappers. Daniel shook his head. The Shawnee, he said, would kill the girls the moment they heard hoofbeats.[2]

Callaway understood that Daniel was right. He and his men struck out for the Licking River to lay an ambush. In camp that night, Daniel saw that his men were not equipped for a long chase. He sent young Gass back for buckskins, food, powder, and shot—and Daniel's moccasins.

By Tuesday, Hanging Maw was forty miles from the river. He was sure he was safe. His warriors killed a buffalo and stopped to cook the hump meat. They did not know that Daniel had outguessed them. As the Shawnee prepared their meal, the rescue party closed in.

The woodsmen were thirty yards away when a lookout spotted them. The men opened fire at once. The Shawnee fled, too startled to think of harming the girls. Daniel fired and saw one of the Shawnee go down. "Run, gals, run!" the men yelled.[3]

A tomahawk whizzed by Betsey's head. A moment later one of the rescuers mistook her for a Shawnee. He was

Daniel Boone tracked his daughter's kidnappers through forty miles of thick woods. He then led a surprise attack that scattered the Shawnee and rescued the girls. A painter later portrayed the famous frontiersman relaxing with his rifle and favorite dog.

~·~·~·~·~✦✦~·~·~·~·~

about to hit her with his rifle butt when Daniel grabbed his arm. "Don't kill her when we've traveled so far to save her," Daniel yelled.[4] A moment later Jemima was safe in his arms.

A month later the people of Boonesborough gathered to witness Betsey's marriage. Daniel had blazed the trail into Kentucky only one year earlier. Now he was an honored guest at the settlement's first wedding.

2

THE CALL OF THE WILDERNESS

Daniel Boone's love of the wilderness was inborn. His grandfather, George Boone, brought the family to America in 1717. From his home in western England, Boone had heard about William Penn's colony. Like Penn, Boone was a member of the Society of Friends—the Quakers. Pennsylvania, reports said, offered cheap land and religious freedom.

At first the Boones settled twelve miles north of Philadelphia. Within a short time they were on the move again. As historian John Bakeless writes, "The Boones were wanderers born. They had the itching foot. . . . They heard of distant lands and knew that they must go there."[1] George Boone's first move took him only a few miles. In 1718 he settled on four hundred acres in Oley Township. The town of Reading grew up nearby.

Boone's son Squire married Sarah Morgan in 1720. Squire was a weaver, but he also hungered to own land. By 1730 he was farming almost four hundred acres of land in Oley. There, on November 2, 1734, Sarah gave birth to her sixth child. The Boones called him Daniel, after Sarah's brother.

The Boone farm lay at the edge of the wilderness. Native American hunters were frequent visitors. Young Daniel made friends with Delaware and Shawnee. Unlike most boys of his time, he studied their way of life. Those

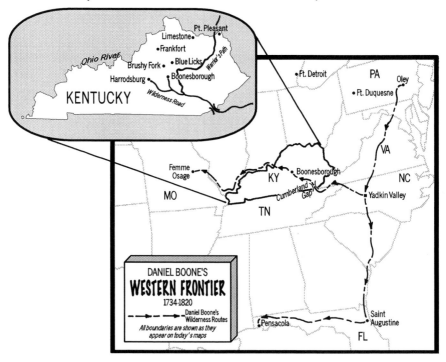

When Daniel Boone was born, only Native Americans roamed the lands west of the Appalachian mountains. Tales of a paradise called Kentucky drew Daniel Boone westward from his home in North Carolina. His courage, skill, and daring helped open the western territories to settlement.

early lessons paid off later. Daniel's skill at thinking like an Indian saved his life more than once.[2]

When Daniel was six, smallpox struck the township. Sarah kept her children at home, hoping they could avoid the dread disease. According to one old story, the confinement did not please young Daniel. The answer, he thought, was to catch smallpox. Once he recovered, he again would be free to wander. One night he sneaked off to a neighbor's farm. There he crawled into bed with a child who was blotched with smallpox sores. As he had planned, the same blotches soon showed up on his skin. Luckily, he and the other Boone children survived the outbreak.[3]

When Daniel was ten, his father bought twenty-five acres of wooded pasture. The land lay some miles from the main farm. Daniel spent the next six summers there with his mother. Their job was to tend the Boones' cattle. Squire stayed home to manage his looms and his blacksmith shop. Daniel's oldest sister cared for the younger children.

By day Daniel roamed the woods as the cattle grazed. At night he drove them home for milking. The boy also helped feed the family. He knew how to find nuts and berries, but hunting was his real passion. Too young to carry a gun, Daniel relied on a throwing stick. Before long he could kill a rabbit at ten yards.[4] His father gave him a short-barreled, muzzle-loading rifle when Daniel was thirteen. Gifted with a keen eye, the boy turned into a top marksman.

The Boones' cows sometimes had to find their own

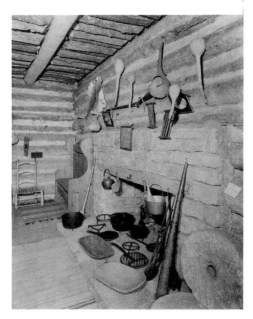

Daniel Boone grew up in backwoods cabins that were furnished much like this reconstructed blockhouse. Life revolved around the fireplace, which provided both heat and light. Settlers brought iron pots and kettles from the East, but made most of their clothing, tools, and furnishings with their own hands.

way home. When hunting was good, Daniel stayed away for days at a time. Sarah worried about him, with good reason. Native American hunters prowled those same woods. The danger excited Daniel. He learned to move through the woods as silently as a shadow. The woods became his schoolroom. Each sight, sound, and smell told him its story.

Daniel never did have much real schooling. Late in life, he told his children that he had never gone to school. A sister-in-law, Sarah Day Boone, taught him to read and write. Years later, a son-in-law polished his skills a little. Despite those efforts, Daniel spelled words the way they sounded. *Copied* became "coppyed." *All right* came out "awl wright." *Business* turned into "bisness."

When his Uncle John complained, Squire had a ready answer. "Let the girls do the spelling and Daniel will do the shooting."[5]

3
A WOODSMAN TAKES A BRIDE

In 1748 the local Quakers expelled Squire Boone. His crime? Two of his children had married non-Quakers. Two years later, Squire sold out and led his family south to North Carolina. He bought 640 acres near the Yadkin River. Land was cheap out on the frontier.

The Boones cleared their fields and planted a corn crop. Daniel hunted deer, turkey, and bear with Tick Licker, his long-barreled flintlock. Legend tells us he could shoot a tick off a bear's snout at one hundred yards. Soon he was staying in the woods for weeks at a time. On the frontier, this was known as a "long hunt." The hides and furs he brought back sold for a good price. After one hunt the teenager spent all his profits "on a general jamboree."[1]

In 1754 British and French forces clashed on the western frontier. The shots signaled the start of the French and

The carvings on this Kentucky long rifle carry the initials DB. If the rifle belonged to Daniel Boone, it might be the hunting rifle he called Tick Licker. It took above average strength and a steady eye to hold and aim this sixty-four-inch, twelve-pound rifle.

Indian War. The British sent General Edward Braddock to take Fort Duquesne from the French. Daniel went along as a wagon driver. He enjoyed the trek through western Pennsylvania. At night, he listened spellbound to John Finley's yarns about far-off Kentucky. The land beyond the Appalachians, Finley told him, was a paradise.

On July 9, Braddock's troops ran into an ambush. French soldiers, fighting beside Iroquois and Shawnee warriors, cut down the advance guard. As war cries echoed in their ears, the British redcoats panicked and fled. Daniel's wagon was caught in the crush. Unable to turn, he jumped on his lead horse and cut the reins. Then he rode for his life.

Soon after his return, Daniel met the love of his life. He first saw Rebecca Bryan at a wedding, but legend tells a more romantic tale. Daniel was hunting deer at night, the story goes. All at once he saw the light of a friend's torch reflected in a pair of startled eyes. As Daniel raised his rifle, a sixth sense told him to hold his fire. In the next instant Rebecca jumped up and ran off through the woods.[2]

Daniel must have chased her, for he married Rebecca on August 14, 1756. She was seventeen, a handsome girl with black hair and dark eyes. The groom was twenty-one. He stood five feet, eight inches tall, with broad shoulders and chest. Piercing blue eyes studied the world from beneath a mop of dark hair. Thin lips framed a large, mobile mouth.[3] His Cherokee friends called him Wide Mouth.

The newlyweds moved into a snug cabin on Sugar Creek. Rebecca proved to be an able helpmate. When

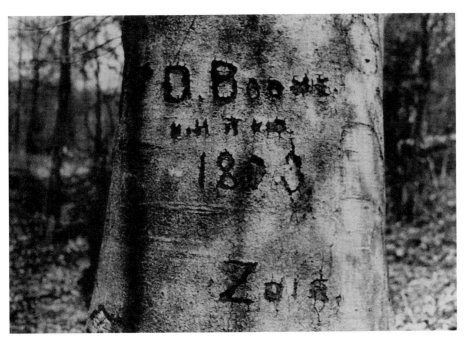

Daniel often marked his passage through a region by carving his name on tree trunks. Hunters found this carving in the woods near modern-day Louisville, Kentucky. The date 1803 fits with Daniel's movements at the time. No one knows what the word "Zois" means.

Rebecca Bryan married Daniel Boone when she was seventeen and he was twenty-one. It was Rebecca who cared for the children and managed the family's affairs during Daniel's lengthy absences. Late in life, when rheumatism robbed Daniel of his agility, Rebecca joined him on his hunting trips to fetch, carry, and cook.

Daniel went hunting, she took over the farmwork. In time, she would also give birth to six sons and four daughters. Their first child, James, was born in 1757.

For ten years the Boones lived a quiet life. Daniel raised crops on what was now a 640-acre farm. In the fall and early winter he left for his long hunts. One hunting trip in 1760 took him into eastern Tennessee. Years later, someone found a beech tree there with deeply inscribed letters. The carving read, *D. Boon cilled a Bar on tree in the year 1760.* Some argue that it is a fake. Daniel, they say, never mis-spelled his own name.[4]

By the mid-1760s Daniel was growing restless. Game was growing scarce as settlers flooded into the Yadkin Valley. In 1765 he trekked to Florida to check out Spain's offer of free land. The hunting was poor, and the swamps bred swarms of insects. Despite these drawbacks, Daniel

For Rebecca Boone, life with her woodsman husband meant saying good-bye at frequent intervals. Daniel cherished his wife and children, but his love of the wilderness led to separations that lasted for months at a time.

talked to Rebecca about moving. She refused to leave her family and friends.

In 1769 John Finley stopped by the Boone cabin. Daniel had not forgotten his friend's stories of Kentucky. Now he wanted to see the paradise for himself. On May 1 Daniel led Finley and four friends westward. The men passed through the Cumberland Gap on a Native American trail called the Warrior's Trace. A few weeks later, Daniel stood on a hilltop north of the Kentucky River. There he gazed for the first time at "the beautiful [land] of Kentucke."[5]

4

"WASPS AND YELLOW JACKETS WILL STING YOU"

The name Kentucky came from the Iroquois word for meadows, *kanta-ke*. Daniel Boone was not the first to glimpse these bluegrass meadows. The Shawnee, Cherokee, and other tribes hunted there. English and French traders had crisscrossed the region for decades.

For six months Daniel's party hunted deer and trapped beaver. All was well until the day a Shawnee war party cornered Daniel and his brother-in-law, John Stewart. The Shawnee soon released their captives, but they took all the skins and horses. With them went the profits of six months labor. The Shawnee leader warned, "If you are so foolish as to venture here again, . . . the wasps and yellow jackets will sting you severely."[1]

The two hunters ignored the warning. For several days

Daniel made his earliest trip through the Cumberland Gap in 1769. A few days later he stood on a hilltop and admired "the beautiful [land] of Kentucke" for the first time. Years later, an artist recreated the moment in this painting.

they tracked the war party. Then, while the Shawnee slept, they stole back their horses. A day later the Shawnee recaptured them. The warriors seemed to enjoy the game. One of them tied a horse collar around Daniel's neck. Then the Shawnee ordered him to dance. When the warriors stopped laughing, they took their captives with them.

A week later the party camped near the Ohio River. That night Daniel and John broke loose. Moving swiftly, they grabbed two rifles and hid in a canebrake. The Shawnee let them go. They were in a rush to get home with their loot.

By this time Finley and the others had fled. Daniel and John went back to trapping. Daniel's brother Squire helped by showing up with fresh supplies. A month later John failed to keep a rendezvous. Daniel's search turned up only the letters *JS* carved on a tree. Five years later a hunter found a skeleton inside a hollow tree. Some jumped to the conclusion that the dead man was John Stewart. Wounded by Shawnee, he may have bled to death in his hiding place.[2]

In May 1770, Squire left to take a load of hides and furs to market. For two months Daniel ranged across Kentucky on his own. Day by day he added to his mental map. The map told him the location of each hill, stream, and salt lick. When he felt lonely, he sang and talked out loud. In July he met Squire at their old camp.

The pair did not head for home until March 1771. Along the way they ran into more bad luck. A band of Cherokee stole their furs, horses, and rifles. For two years, Daniel wrote, he had not tasted salt, sugar, or bread.[3] Now he returned to the Yadkin Valley empty-handed and in debt. He had paid for his supplies with borrowed money.

All this time, Americans were pushing beyond the mountains. A British law had forbidden this movement, but it could not be enforced. In 1773 a wealthy Virginia landowner named William Russell caught the Kentucky fever. He picked Daniel to lead his expedition.

Rebecca gave birth to their eighth child that spring. A few months later, the whole Boone family set out for Kentucky. A number of Boones and Bryans joined the party. Each group took only what could be carried on pack-horses. Small children rode in baskets tied to the saddles.

The party made slow progress. Daniel had to send back for more supplies. His sixteen-year-old son, James, rode with the supply train. On October 9, a Delaware war party fired on the party as the men lay sleeping. The first shots killed two men and wounded James Boone and Henry Russell. The warriors then stormed into the camp and tortured the helpless teenagers. The two boys died slowly and in great pain.

The settlers lost heart when they learned of the four deaths. Daniel buried his son and returned home. He had no crops to harvest. To feed his family, he hunted all through the winter. In the spring he returned to Kentucky to visit his son's grave.

The killings sparked a small war. White gunmen killed a number of blameless Native Americans. Shawnee and Cherokee warriors struck back. Daniel, now a militia lieutenant, took charge of several frontier forts. The people who took shelter there trusted his leadership. By the time the fighting ended in the fall, he had risen to captain.

5
THE WILDERNESS ROAD

When Daniel was unable to repay his debts, the lenders took him to court. To defend himself, he turned to lawyer Richard Henderson. When they met, Daniel often described Kentucky's wonders to the wealthy North Carolinian.

Henderson listened carefully. In 1775 he formed the Transylvania Company as a way of speculating in western lands. Before he could do so, he had to gain title to the land. The lawyer's solution was to open talks with the Cherokee. The fact that the tribe did not own the land did not stop him. Neither did the fact that he was breaking the law. Since 1763 settlers had been confined to the lands east of the Appalachians.

It was Daniel who arranged the meeting. Over a thousand Cherokee gathered in March 1775 for the talks.

Henderson won their good will by showing up with six wagons full of trade goods. He claimed the cargo was worth $50,000. Some observers did not believe him. They saw mostly "cheap trinkets," firearms, and rum.[1]

After much debate, the Cherokee sold 20 million acres. The land lay between the Kentucky and Cumberland rivers. Henderson also won the right to open a road to his land. Most of the Cherokee leaders signed the Great Grant. One who did not was a chief named Dragging Canoe. "Brother, we have given you a fine land," he warned Daniel. "But . . . you will have much trouble in settling it."[2]

Daniel left the meeting early. Henderson had offered him two thousand acres of prime land. In payment, Daniel had promised to open a road into Kentucky. His friends and neighbors hurried to join him. The pay was good—ten British pounds (£10) to each workman. As a bonus, they could pick the best land for themselves.

The roadbuilders met on

Building forts, homes, and farms in the wilderness required cooperative effort. It was skilled axmen like these fencebuilders who worked alongside Daniel Boone in opening the first pack trail into Kentucky.

the Virginia-North Carolina border. Squire was there. So was Daniel's daughter Susannah and her new husband. Fourteen-year-old Susannah had hired on to cook and keep camp. It was a good time for Daniel to be away from home. In mid-April a creditor swore out a warrant for his arrest. The sheriff tried, but could not serve the court papers. Across the back he scrawled, "Gone to Kentucky."[3]

Daniel marked the way along the Warrior's Trace. The first trees fell to the woodsmen's axes on March 10, 1775. Yard by yard, the men carved a pack trail through the wilderness. They cleared brush and dug out rocks. They slashed their way through canebrakes. Snow and sleet slowed the work, but did not stop it. Henderson later wrote that "no part of the road [was] tolerable." Most of the Wilderness Road was hilly, stony, or muddy.[4]

Two weeks of backbreaking labor took the crew into Kentucky. Certain that the worst was over, the workers camped near a boiling spring. On March 24, they awoke to the sound of gunfire. Dragging Canoe's prophecy was coming true. As Daniel described it, "A party of Indians fired on my company about half an hour before day. [They] killed Mr. Twetty and his negro."[5] A second attack two days later cost two more lives.

Only Daniel's cool courage kept the men from fleeing. On April 6 the weary party reached journey's end. Daniel led them to a site on the south bank of the Kentucky River. There the men built a cluster of log huts. A rude, unfinished

The site that Daniel chose beside the Kentucky River quickly grew into a fortified settlement called Boonesborough. The future was bright in this fertile, well-watered land, but the present was less promising. The cabins were damp and drafty, food was scarce, and Native American war parties lay in wait for unwary hunters.

twelve-foot stockade guarded the enclosure. The men called it Fort Boone.

Daniel resolved to bring his family to Kentucky. He felt sure his tiny settlement would grow. His workers, too, were pleased with their prospects. Indeed, their hunger for land caused a problem. The men left the fort unguarded while they scrambled to stake their claims.

Henderson's caravan of packhorses arrived two weeks later. With them came seeds, trade goods, black powder, and cattle. Henderson renamed the site Boonesborough. He later wrote, "It was owing to Boone's confidence in us and the people's in him that a stand was ever attempted."[6]

6

RUNNING THE GAUNTLET

～～～～～～～▲ ～～～～～～

The first shots of the American Revolution rang out on April 19, 1776. In Kentucky, the settlers cheered the news. Then they turned back to their own problems.

The Transylvania Company refused to allow free elections. Worse still, it planned to charge settlers a yearly rent for each acre farmed. Daniel was worried about the lack of game. He pushed for a rule to keep hunters from killing for sport.[1]

Back East, the company met more setbacks. The Continental Congress refused to make Kentucky the fourteenth colony. Virginia, in turn, declared that Kentucky was one of its counties. The company was forced to focus on other land grants. It never did give Daniel all of the acres he had been promised.

In September, Daniel led a second pack train to Boonesborough. Rebecca and seven of their children were at his side. The hardships of frontier life were waiting for the newcomers.

Food was scarce. The crude cabins were damp and drafty. The Shawnee were on the warpath. Even so, the pack trains kept coming. Over five hundred settlers now lived in Kentucky.

In August 1776, a rider brought news of the Declaration of Independence. The British struck back against the colonists. Their agents urged the Shawnee to mount new raids. The threat sent settlers running for safety. By year's end, only 150 riflemen remained in all of Kentucky.[2]

In April 1777, a war party caught twelve settlers outside the fort. Daniel was one of them. "Boys, we have to fight!" Daniel yelled. "Sell your lives as dear as possible!"[3]

Daniel led a charge through the band of Shawnee. Just as a path opened, a rifle ball shattered his ankle. As Daniel fell, a Shawnee jumped on him. Simon Kenton shot the warrior and crushed a second Shawnee's skull with his gun barrel. Then he hoisted Daniel to his shoulders and ran for the fort. The Shawnee withdrew when the gates slammed shut.

By January 1778, the salt used for preserving food was running low. Daniel, his ankle well healed, led thirty men to the spring at Blue Licks. There the other men made salt by boiling the briny water in iron kettles. Daniel did the hunting.

On February 7, four Shawnee captured Daniel during a snowstorm. Back at the Shawnee camp, Daniel saw the size of the war party and shivered. Boonesborough surely would fall if the Shawnee attacked. Daniel hit on a plan to

George Caleb Bingham captured the central drama of Daniel's life in this oil painting. Known as "Daniel Boone Escorting Settlers Through the Cumberland Gap," it shows Daniel leading the column with his rifle at the ready. The great frontiersman was passing into legend by the time Bingham captured this scene in the early 1850s.

trade the salt-boiling party for the safety of those at the fort. The lure of an easy victory appealed to Blackfish, the Shawnee leader. He knew the British would pay £20 for each captive. A day later, Daniel approached his men and explained his plan. They agreed to lay down their arms.

Blackfish led his captives northward. One night, as a test of courage, he forced Daniel to run the gauntlet. The Shawnee stood in two long lines. They were armed with clubs, sticks, and tomahawks. Daniel ran a zigzag path that evaded many of the blows. A stumble could have meant his death. At the end of the line, a warrior stepped in front of him, tomahawk raised. Daniel put his head down and rammed the man in the chest. Blackfish was so pleased that he later adopted Daniel.

In 1778, Daniel saved Boonesborough from attack by allowing himself and his salt-making party to be taken prisoner. The Shawnee marched the woodsmen to Fort Detroit to show off their captives to the British. At last, when the Shawnee relaxed their vigilance, Daniel managed to escape. He raced through 160 miles of heavy forest to warn the fort of an impending assault.

At Fort Detroit, Blackfish introduced Daniel as his new son. Daniel showed Governor Hamilton his British militia commission. Then he hinted that the Kentucky settlers were loyal to King George. The lie may have fooled the British. Blackfish, however, was planning a new attack on Boonesborough.

It was June before the Shawnee relaxed their guard. When they did, Daniel made his escape. After he shook off pursuit he headed for Boonesborough. Four days and 160 miles later, he stood in front of the gates. In his Shawnee dress no one knew him at first. Even his looks had changed. Blackfish had plucked out his hair, leaving only a topknot.

7

BOONESBOROUGH UNDER SIEGE

Only Jemima rushed to welcome her father when Daniel returned to Boonesborough. Rebecca had taken the other children back to North Carolina. She thought her husband was dead. Daniel set that problem aside and turned to the task of fighting the Shawnee. Under his command, the men strengthened the fort's defenses. The women stockpiled food and bandages. Outside the stockade, a crew cleared the brush. Riflemen needed a clear field of fire.

The work stopped on September 7, 1778. A unit of British militia troops from Canada had appeared outside Boonesborough. With them were Blackfish and four hundred Shawnee.

Blackfish called on the fort to surrender. In return, he promised safe passage to Detroit. Wary of promises, the men in the fort voted to fight.

Daniel and Squire relayed the message to Blackfish. They also gave him false reports on the fort's strength. To support the deception, the women dressed like men and carried rifles.

The talks dragged on. On September 11, Blackfish offered a peace treaty. After both sides signed, Daniel reached to shake the chief's hand. Blackfish grabbed his arm and tried to drag him away. As the men struggled, both sides opened fire. In the confusion Daniel managed to make a mad dash to safety.[1]

For two days each side blazed away. Then the siege force tried a new tactic. Blackfish put his braves to work on a tunnel. If it worked, the tunnel would undermine the fort's walls. While the digging went on, the Shawnee set cabin roofs ablaze with fire arrows.

At that dark moment it started to rain. The downpour did more than put out the fires. The rain-soaked earth caved in the tunnel.

Boonesborough barely survived a September 1778 attack by four hundred Shawnee warriors. When trickery failed to win the day, Chief Blackfish and his men opened fire with rifles and fire arrows. The Shawnee broke off the attack after a heavy rain collapsed the tunnel they were digging under the fort's walls.

With that, the Shawnee broke the siege and slipped away. The settlers rejoiced in their triumph. They later claimed to have killed thirty-seven Shawnee, while losing only two of their own.[2]

Daniel did not have time to savor the victory. A few hotheads blamed him for the surrender of the salt-boilers. Now they added the charge of treason. He had been too friendly with the British, they said. In October, Daniel stood trial at a court-martial.

He had no choice but to sidetrack the Shawnee, Daniel told the court. If he had failed, the fort would have fallen. Women and children would have been massacred. Upon his escape, he pointed out, he went back to the fort. There he stayed, to be "tomahawked and shot, . . . and to risk his very life to save them."[3] The court found him not guilty. It also promoted him to the rank of major.

A year later Daniel brought his family back to Kentucky. He settled Rebecca and the children at Boone's Station, five miles north of Boonesborough. That winter Daniel went to Virginia to buy more land for himself and some friends. In James City, thieves stole $20,000 from his saddlebags. Once again, he had lost everything.

Daniel worked hard to earn back the stolen money. He served as sheriff of Fayette County and as a deputy surveyor. In April 1781 his neighbors sent him to serve in the Virginia Assembly. At Charlottesville he was captured and released by British troops. In October the British surrendered at Yorktown. The fighting in the East was over.

The settlers won the long struggle to claim Kentucky, but they paid a high price. Daniel's son Israel was one of the young men who died in the Battle of Blue Licks in 1782. In this old engraving, Daniel turns from Israel just in time to defend himself against an onrushing Shawnee.

~:~:~:~:~◣ ◢~:~:~:~:~

The war on the frontier lasted longer. In August 1782 Daniel helped turn back the Shawnee in the Battle of Blue Licks. The victory was dearly won. His son Israel died in his arms during the battle.

A final skirmish with the Shawnee had a happier ending. In 1783 Daniel was hanging tobacco to dry in a small shed. As he climbed up the drying racks, four Shawnee burst in. "Now, Boone, we got you. You no get away more," one of them called.[4]

Daniel was not one to panic. He smiled and chatted with his "old friends," all the while gathering an armload of dried tobacco. When the braves were off guard, he threw the tobacco in their faces. As he had hoped, the dust blinded the Shawnee. Daniel slipped out of the shed and ran to safety.

8
CIVILIZATION CLOSES IN

In 1783 Daniel was nearing his fiftieth birthday. If he hoped to live a quiet life, those hopes were soon blasted. A sheriff came to Boone's Station to tell Daniel that he would have to move. His land, the court papers said, belonged to someone else.

Dismayed but not daunted, Daniel moved his family to Limestone, Kentucky. Settlers traveling by flatboat entered Kentucky through the tiny settlement on the Ohio River. Limestone "is become a grate Landing place," Daniel noted.[1] Before long the Boones owned a wharf, a warehouse, a store, and a tavern. Travelers ate Rebecca's meals and slept in a back room.

Over the next three years, Daniel made over a hundred surveys. Clients paid him with pieces of the land he surveyed. Daniel followed the custom of the day. He described boundaries in terms of landmarks such as trees and streams. When he finished a survey, Daniel promised clear title to the land. Then, more woodsman than lawyer, he often failed to do all the paperwork. When the courts took their land away, many of his clients sued Daniel.

In 1784 a backwoods teacher named John Filson published a history of Kentucky. Only a brief final section, "The Adventures of Colonel Daniel Boon," caught the public eye. The thirty-four pages were based on Filson's talks with Daniel. Popular in America, the book was a sensation in Europe. No one seemed to care that the story was full of tall tales. What did Daniel think? Perhaps he had a twinkle in his eye when he said, "All true! . . . Not a lie in it!"[2]

Authors and painters featured Daniel in their works. On paper, it appeared that the new hero was a rich man. He had some one hundred thousand acres under claim. He owned a business and three slaves. He was in demand as a surveyor. His land titles, however, were in dispute. Land sharks took him to court. They contested his right to thousands of acres. Some of his business ventures failed. His name sold books, but no one paid him a share of the profits.

After six years at Limestone, Daniel moved upstream to Point Pleasant. He opened a store there. Customers seldom found him behind the counter. Surveying, guiding newcomers, and selling horses filled his days. He was happiest when he was hunting and trapping. His friends, he found, still trusted him. They sent him east to serve a second term

Daniel was recognized as a national hero by the time Chester Harding painted this portrait in 1819. Despite his eighty-five years, Daniel's gaze is steady and his mouth firm. It is the only portrait of the frontiersman known to have been painted from life.

in the Virginia Assembly. The state put him in command of the local militia.

In 1792 the United States welcomed Kentucky as its fifteenth state. It was a time for merchants and farmers, not woodsmen. Daniel was feeling the weight of his years. His joints ached. He was still an avid hunter, but now Rebecca traveled with him to keep camp. In 1795 the Boones moved thirty miles west to Brushy Fork. Daniel and his youngest son, Nathan, built a one-room cabin. Four of their married daughters lived nearby.

Legal judgments trickled in. By 1789 Daniel had lost most of his land. In the fall a sheriff came to arrest him for failing to appear in court. The lawman went home empty-handed. Daniel had given up his land claims and moved far upriver. He told his children that "he would rather be poor than retain an acre of land . . . so long as claims and debts hung over him."[3]

After they moved to Missouri, Daniel and Rebecca could have lived in their son Nathan's fine home. They preferred this small cabin in the Femme Osage District. By the time this photo was taken, time and weather had conspired to reduce the once-stout cabin to near ruin.

Out west, Spain needed settlers to farm the empty land that is now called Missouri. Daniel accepted Governor Zenon Trudeau's offer of 850 acres. Trudeau knew that where Daniel went, others would follow. Daniel and Rebecca headed west in 1799. They brought with them a flock of sons, daughters, and grandchildren. Daniel walked every step of the seven hundred miles.

The Boones settled in the Femme Osage District near the Missouri River. In June 1800 Daniel was appointed to new duties as a syndic. A syndic was sheriff, judge, and jury all in one. Daniel held court under a tall elm known as the Judgment Tree. No one ever appealed his decisions.

9

A MOST
UNCOMMON MAN

In 1800 Spain ceded the Louisiana Territory to France. Three years later, France sold Louisiana to the United States. The transfer left all Missouri land claims in doubt. To hold his land, Daniel should have been living on it and farming it. Busy with his duties, he had done neither. To keep the family close, he and Rebecca had lived on a son's land.

The Spanish, Daniel argued, had excused syndics from the rules. The laws of the United States, however, did not recognize Spanish customs. An American land commission denied his claim. The courts backed the commission. In 1810, at age seventy-five, Daniel found himself landless and nearly broke.[1]

The War of 1812 renewed the struggle between the United States and Great Britain. Daniel was one of the first to volunteer. He was certain his knowledge of frontier warfare would be needed. The army turned him down.

That same year, Daniel asked Congress to restore his 8,500 acres. Kentucky's senators did their best, but Congress was slow to act. Two years passed before Daniel's land was restored. Even then, he was shortchanged. Congress gave him only 850 acres, a tenth of what he claimed.[2]

By that time, Daniel was grieving over the death of his wife. Rebecca died in 1813 at age seventy-four. A granddaughter said he had suffered "the Saddest affliction of his life."[3] Even the return of his 850 acres gave Daniel little cheer. The news brought old creditors out to press their bills. Daniel paid the claims by selling the land. "I have paid all my debts," he told his family. "No one will say when I am gone, 'Boone was a dishonest man.' "[4]

Old age did not rob Daniel of his love of the outdoors. He made his last long hunt sometime around 1810. On that trek Daniel hunted and trapped along Wyoming's Yellowstone River. Back home, he complained that Missouri was filling up. He talked about heading west, perhaps to California.

As the years passed, the old woodsman contented himself with smaller joys. He sang to his grandchildren and told them stories. Shawnee friends came by to visit. He repaired rifles, carved powder horns, and sewed moccasins. His mind was still sharp. A visitor asked him if he had ever been lost. "No, I was never lost," Daniel shot back. "But I was bewildered once for three days."[5]

In 1845, Kentucky brought Daniel and Rebecca home for burial in the state capital at Frankfurt. A second notable memorial stands in a park in Lexington. This heroic bronze statue captures the courage and vision that earned Daniel a place of honor on the roster of America's pioneers.

His death came on September 26, 1820, after a brief illness. The crowd that came to the funeral overflowed Jemima's house. Services had to be held out back, in the barn. Ever since Rebecca's death, Daniel had kept his coffin ready. His family used it to bury him beside her.

In 1845 Kentucky had a change of heart. The state that had driven him out now wanted him back. Daniel and Rebecca were reburied at Frankfurt, Kentucky. There they lie today beneath a marble monument.

The legends about Daniel have grown taller than his monument. Books and films have credited him with superhuman feats. If the great pioneer were alive today, he would set the record straight. "Many heroic . . . adventures are related of me which exist only in the regions of fancy," Daniel once told a visitor. "With me the world has taken great liberties, and yet I have been but a common man."[6]

No one who knows the true story would agree. Daniel Boone was one of this nation's most *uncommon* men.

CHAPTER NOTES

Chapter 1

1. Lawrence Elliott, *The Long Hunter: A New Life of Daniel Boone* (New York: Readers Digest Press, 1976), pp. 102–103.

2. John Bakeless, *Daniel Boone* (Harrisburg, Pa.: Stackpole Co., 1939), p. 131.

3. Ibid., p. 135.

4. John Mack Faragher, *Daniel Boone: The Life and Legend of an American Pioneer* (New York: Henry Holt and Co., 1992), p. 137.

Chapter 2

1. John Bakeless, *Daniel Boone* (Harrisburg, Pa.: Stackpole Co., 1939), p. 5.

2. Ibid., p. 9.

3. Lawrence Elliott, *The Long Hunter: A New Life of Daniel Boone* (New York: Readers Digest Press, 1976), p. 9.

4. Ibid., pp. 13–14.

5. Bakeless, p. 11.

Chapter 3

1. John Mack Faragher, *Daniel Boone: The Life and Legend of an American Pioneer* (New York: Henry Holt and Co., 1992), pp. 28–29.

2. Ibid., pp. 43–44.

3. Michael Lofaro, *The Life and Adventures of Daniel Boone* (Lexington, Ky.: University of Kentucky Press, 1978), p. 14.

4. John Bakeless, *Daniel Boone* (Harrisburg, Pa.: Stackpole Co., 1939), pp. 32–33.

5. Faragher, p. 79.

Chapter 4

1. John Mack Faragher, *Daniel Boone: The Life and Legend of an American Pioneer* (New York: Henry Holt and Co., 1992), p. 81.

2. Lawrence Elliott, *The Long Hunter: A New Life of Daniel Boone* (New York: Readers Digest Press, 1976), p. 61.

3. Cecil B. Hartley, *Life of Daniel Boone* (Philadelphia: Porter & Coates, 1865), p. 28.

Chapter 5

1. John Mack Faragher, *Daniel Boone: The Life and Legend of an American Pioneer* (New York: Henry Holt and Co., 1992), p. 111.

2. John Bakeless, *Daniel Boone* (Harrisburg, Pa.: Stackpole Co., 1939), p. 87.

3. Ibid., p. 90.

4. Faragher, p. 114.

5. John S. Abbot, *Daniel Boone: Pioneer of Kentucky* (New York: Dodd, Mead and Co., 1872), p. 51.

6. Faragher, p. 118.

Chapter 6

1. John Bakeless, *Daniel Boone* (Harrisburg, Pa.: Stackpole Co., 1939), p. 104.

2. Michael Lofaro, *The Life and Adventures of Daniel Boone* (Lexington, Ky.: University of Kentucky Press, 1978), p. 66.

3. John Mack Faragher, *Daniel Boone: The Life and Legend of an American Pioneer* (New York: Henry Holt and Co., 1992), p. 148.

Chapter 7

1. John Mack Faragher, *Daniel Boone: The Life and Legend of an American Pioneer* (New York: Henry Holt and Co., 1992), pp. 191–192.

2. W. H. Bogart, *The Border Boy and How He Became the Great Pioneer of the West; A Life of Daniel Boone* (Boston: Lee and Shepard, Publishers, 1884), p. 230.

3. Lawrence Elliott, *The Long Hunter: A New Life of Daniel Boone* (New York: Readers Digest Press, 1976), pp. 153–154.

4. Bogart, p. 298.

Chapter 8

1. John Mack Faragher, *Daniel Boone: The Life and Legend of an American Pioneer* (New York: Henry Holt and Co., 1992), p. 235.

2. John Bakeless, *Daniel Boone* (Harrisburg, Pa.: Stackpole Co., 1939), p. 395.

3. Faragher, pp. 269–270.

Chapter 9

1. George C. Hill, *Daniel Boone: The Pioneer of Kentucky* (Philadelphia: Claxton, Remsen & Haffelfinger, 1869), pp. 250–251.

2. Lawrence Elliott, *The Long Hunter: A New Life of Daniel Boone* (New York: Readers Digest Press, 1976), pp. 197–198.

3. John Mack Faragher, *Daniel Boone: The Life and Legend of an American Pioneer* (New York: Henry Holt and Co., 1992), p. 307.

4. Ibid., p. 308.

5. John Bakeless, *Daniel Boone* (Harrisburg, Pa.: Stackpole Co., 1939), p. 413.

6. Faragher, p. 302.

GLOSSARY

ambush—A sudden attack made from a concealed position.

assembly—The lower chamber of a state legislature.

buckskins—Pants and jackets made from the tanned hide of a male deer.

canebrake—A dense thicket made up of reeds or bamboo.

commission—A government document that appoints someone to a particular rank or office.

Continental Congress—The legislative body that governed the newly independent colonies until 1789.

court-martial—A court that tries officers and enlisted personnel who have been accused of crimes under military law.

flatboat—A raftlike boat with a cabin on the deck.

flintlock—A firearm in which a flint embedded in the hammer produces a spark. The spark, in turn, ignites a powder charge and fires the weapon.

frontier—A region just being opened to settlers.

gauntlet—Men armed with sticks or other weapons arrange themselves in two lines and try to hit the person forced to run between them. Running the gauntlet can be a form of punishment or a test of courage.

legend—A story that many people believe, but which is often untrue in whole or in part.

militia—Part-time soldiers who are called to duty in times of emergency.

moccasins—The soft leather shoes worn by Native Americans. Woodsmen adopted moccasins as their standard footware.

pioneers—The men and women who open a wilderness area to settlement.

pound (£)—The British monetary unit. The American colonists used the pound as their currency in the years before the American Revolution.

powder horn—A cow horn used for carrying gunpowder. To make a powder horn, a woodsman hollowed out a cow horn, capped it, and decorated it with carved designs.

salt lick—A natural deposit of salt that animals come from miles around to lick.

scalps—Portions of the skin and hair cut from human heads. On the frontier, both Native Americans and settlers took scalps as battle trophies.

siege—An attack on a town or fortress that traps the defenders within their fortified positions.

speculator—Someone who engages in risky ventures in hopes of making a quick profit.

stockade—An enclosed area walled with sharpened stakes.

surveyor—Someone who determines the boundaries of a plot of land by measuring angles and distances from known landmarks.

syndic—A civil official appointed by the Spanish to conduct legal and judicial business.

tomahawk—A light, short-handled ax used as a weapon by many Native American tribes.

trail signs—The traces left by humans and animals as they move through a wilderness area.

trapper—Someone who makes a living by catching fur-bearing animals in traps.

treason—The act of betraying one's country by giving aid to its enemies.

warrant—A legal paper that authorizes a law enforcement officer to make a search or an arrest, or to execute a judgment.

MORE GOOD READING ABOUT
DANIEL BOONE

Bakeless, John. *Daniel Boone*. Harrisburg, Pa.: Stackpole Co., 1939.

Bogart, W. H. *The Border Boy and How He Became the Great Pioneer of the West: A Life of Daniel Boone*. Boston: Lee and Shepard, Publishers, 1884.

Cavan, Seamus. *Daniel Boone and the Opening of the Ohio Country*. New York: Chelsea House Publishers, 1991.

Elliott, Lawrence. *The Long Hunter: A New Life of Daniel Boone*. New York: Readers Digest Press, 1976.

Faragher, John Mack. *Daniel Boone: The Life and Legend of an American Pioneer*. New York: Henry Holt and Co., 1992.

Lawlor, Laurie. *Daniel Boone*. Niles, Ill.: Albert Whitman & Co., 1989.

Lofaro, Michael. *The Life and Adventures of Daniel Boone*. Lexington, Ky.: University of Kentucky Press, 1978.

INDEX